MIRROR

Take pattern by the moon, O monks,
When ye go abegging.
Samyutta-Nikāya

The moon is the mother of pathos and pity
Wallace Stevens

MIRROR
FOR THE MOON

A SELECTION OF POEMS
BY SAIGYŌ (1118–1190)

TRANSLATED WITH AN INTRODUCTION
BY WILLIAM R. LaFLEUR

FOREWORD BY GARY SNYDER

A NEW DIRECTIONS BOOK

Earlier versions of some of the translations in this volume first appeared in *The Denver Quarterly* and *Kuksu*.

The epigraph from Wallace Stevens's "Lunar Park," in *The Collected Poems of Wallace Stevens* (Copyright © 1954 by Wallace Stevens) is reprinted by permission of Alfred A. Knopf, Inc.

Manufactured in the United States of America
First published clothbound and as New Directions Paperbook 465 in 1978
Published simultaneously in Canada by George J. McLeod Ltd., Toronto

Library of Congress Cataloging in Publication Data

Saigyō, 1118-1190.
   Mirror for the moon.
   (A New Directions Book)
   Translation of selections from Sankashū.
   Bibliography: p. 93
   Includes index.
   I. LaFleur, William R.   II. Title.
PL788.5.S22E5 1978   895.6'1'1   78–5952
ISBN 0–8112–0698–x
ISBN 0–8112–0699–8 pbk.

New Directions Books are published for James Laughlin
by New Directions Publishing Corporation,
80 Eighth Avenue, New York 10011

SECOND PRINTING

CONTENTS

For my grandfathers,
    John, who walked me through the streets of Paterson,
    Sipp, who walked me through his gardens of flowers—
Good memories of good men.

                    Kyoto
                    o-bon   1977

FOREWORD

What is all this about—the moon and flowers? Saigyō the monk-poet traveled wide and far. His poems speak of monkeys, owls, fishermen, boulders, emptiness, love, war, the Buddha-dharma, and old acquaintances of Kyoto days; but most seem to keep coming back to the moon, watched from hundreds of places, hundreds of nights. And Saigyō keeps returning in poem and in body to the flowering cherry, sakura, especially the trees that bloom on the hills of Yoshino.

Some of the power in these poems—in Japanese and in these translations—comes from the way the web of attention is spun out on a complex syntax, drawing the mind as far as it will stretch, to be deftly completed with a final phrase that sometimes illuminates all that went before. The effort is meditative, and though the poems look short they go a long way. Haiku, as a shorter form developed later, is a confession that waka, Saigyō's form, is difficult to sustain. Haiku, with fewer syllables, moves more quickly; it has even more immediacy, less "mind" in the way. Yet, Saigyō's waka are as necessary to haiku, and to the mind, as sutras are to koans; as organic evolution is to the cricket of the moment.

So, Saigyō's fifty-year-long Buddhist practice was gazing at moon and flowers, while being in many places. To anyone who has moved on similar paths, it is clear that Saigyō had in fact entered deeply into nature in an experiential way. He was not writing—as some have suggested—merely to a faddish mode. No temple-bound monk could write of climbing a cliff clutching wild azaleas, or of wading a deep river and feeling "washed clean to the base of the heart." The richness of his knowledge of watersheds, seasonal cycles, and organisms brings one back again to the question, why all those moons and flowers?

Moonlight has been pouring down on this planet for billions of years, and for all us beings tuned to—nay, fed by, the energy of the sun, the light of the moon has long been an odd and unsettling force. We have it inside us, like seawater and calcium, a cool light that is always in motion, but stable and recurrent in its changes. The full moon has long been a Buddhist symbol of the Tathagata; of perfect and complete enlightenment. Even enlightenment may be understood as just a fine high phase in a cycle—who does not also love the sight of the new crescent moon in a lavender sunset sky? But Saigyō takes the moon into his mind and out again, it is an opening into another way of seeing this universe in all its space and with its beautiful fragile little creatures.

Though Saigyō wouldn't have thought much about it, the flowers of flowering plants co-evolved with insects and are beautiful and sweet-scented for them, not for human beings. The flowering cherries of Japan—*Prunus serrulata* and relatives—produce negligible fruit and are closer to a wild type, the mountain sakura, that blooms on the dark conifer hillsides like gleaming clouds. There are a trembling, expectant several days of open-ness—waiting for the seed to move around—and then they blow off and away. Saigyō says, as if he himself were a bee drawn to the flower, that the masses of blossoms on the slopes of Yoshino mountain draw him to the depths of the hills, for knowledge:

> Yoshino mountains—
> The one who will get to know
>   You inside-out is I,
> For I've gotten used to going
> Into your depths for blossoms.

The blossoms then are also a way into the inner depths, as well as the more commonly taken symbol of evanescence and youthful beauty.

Some friends and I once hiked through the Yoshino hills at just that time of spring—cherries are still there, pouring down from the heights "like a cascade of white cloud." We went on, up the old mountain-yogin's trail, and traversed the whole sacred ridge of Ōmine for four days. Many Japanese readers will know that above and behind Yoshino is the oldest center of Mountain Buddhist practice in the country, a landscape mandala in which Ōmine Peak is the center of the Diamond Realm.

A sense of fleeting life and tiny size in vast calm void on the arm of the curve of the planet makes us also bugs in a realm of flowers. No judgments are made, but through those gazing meditations lies a compassionate, broad view. The moments of loneliness and vacillation ("a warbler lost in a cloud!") are not only human, but correct. We and nature are companions; and although authoritative voices do not speak from clouds, a vast, subtle music surrounds us, accessible via clarity and serenity.

All that Saigyō left behind was his poems. There is a modest Japanese restaurant in Sacramento, California, called Kagetsu, "Flowers and Moon." It would be called something else, and there might be no cherry trees planted in Washington, D.C., if Saigyō hadn't lived. There is also the terribly overcrowded, polluted, successful, and confused modern Japan.

Saigyō's poems are masterful mind-language challenges. Bill LaFleur's deeply understanding translations present us with the snake-like energy of the syntax, and the illuminated world that was called out by one man's lifetime of walking and meditating is again right here.

GARY SNYDER

INTRODUCTION

When Matsuo Bashō, the seventeenth-century poet usually considered to be Japan's best, thought about his debt to past masters, he chose Saigyō as the classic poet to whom he owed most. Bashō wrote that the reason for this selection was that he found in the twelfth-century poet "a mind both obeying and at one with nature throughout the four seasons." Saigyō had written in the classic thirty-one-syllable form called "waka," whereas Bashō took up and perfected the more recently evolved seventeen-syllable haiku form. Yet there is something similar in the way both poets approached nature. Bashō's phrase about obedience to, and union with, nature really states it very well. We can detect in their verse an attitude of awe *combined* with intimacy—without the customary response according to the size or scale of the phenomenon. In Saigyō's and Bashō's verses the cricket and the frog can be worthy of reverence; distant mountains and the moon become close companions in some sense. Still, theirs was not an arbitrary or merely clever suspension of ordinary ways of assigning values. These two poets held that the "ordinary" divisions are deceptive, because when natural phenomena are really comprehended, reasons for awe can be found in the pith of what is most familiar and intimacy at the core of what most astonishes.

This sense that the reasons for awe and for intimacy come together at the inner penetralia of things derived, at least in part, from Buddhist philosophy. But in Saigyō and Bashō a discontent with the "ordinary" perceptions and conceptions of society came as well from the pilgrimages each took, the long and sometimes excruciating journeys they insisted upon making into the mountainous countryside of Japan. Their notion was that it was necessary to put both body and mind on the back road in order to emerge out of those deeply rutted and worn conventions of life and habits of mind which they simply called the "world" or "society." These journeys were made to break the charm of those social practices that mask what the Buddhists called the truth of "codependent origination." But they were also intended to remove the cataracts of custom from eyes needing to see new possibilities for poetry.

Nevertheless, five hundred years separated Saigyō from Bashō; they lived in very different kinds of times. Bashō, who lived in the more settled and peaceful era, knew much more fame as a poet during his lifetime. His problem came in part from this renown. The "world" pressed in on him so that he found it occlusive to his vision. This was reason enough to seek the back roads to refresh his perspective. Saigyō, by contrast, lived in very troubled times—at a point in history when, although they were stumbling into the night of extinction, his contemporaries refused to see that they were at the dying end of a glorious era and acted as if things remained as they had been. Saigyō saw and recorded their folly— while celebrating the fact that he found no comparable derangement in the natural world.

In our own century Japanese scholars have had to sift through the received accounts of Saigyō's life, since what seemed reliable came down to them mixed with medieval legend and hagiography. The result of this analysis has been that Saigyō has easily retained his reputation as a poet with an extraordinary vision of the natural world, the quality Bashō so admired. But a less expected outcome has been the emergence from the reliable materials of a Saigyō who, in ways contrasting both with his contemporaries and with Bashō as well, reflected directly on events and trends in the society of his day—in a word, a poet who was much more aware of historical processes than the medieval portraits of him as merely a recluse monk had given reason to suspect. The headnotes he affixed to his poems were unusual for his time; sometimes lengthy and often personal, they include poignant reflections on the madness that Saigyō saw surfacing in public life. The irony is that we learn more about the times from this monk-poet who intentionally put distance between himself and what he called the "world" than we do from the poetry of his contemporaries who went on living in the midst of the national capital, writing verses on set themes as if their society were not, in fact, falling apart.

What needs understanding is the specific contour of Saigyō's mind and imagination—the specific nexus there between the baleful eye he opened on the society of his time and the receptive and sharp one he opened to the natural world. For it is clear that he was no misanthrope; the society he criticized was also one he knew intimately and often yearned for when isolated from it. Nor was his life in the mountains easy. The loneliness he suffered there was like a long and recurring illness, the fevers of which made his mind and eyes fix on the natural world around him until, with an ecstasy he records, he was able to pass into what he regarded as its own inner, restorative, calm. He writes of having practiced Buddhist disciplines often in the mountains—very likely meditations, one type of which at that time involved long and steady contemplation of the moon. Saigyō insisted that through all this he had discovered in nature what he called a "depth" completely beyond the ken of people passing their lives in society. But before considering what this might have meant, it is necessary to sketch briefly his times and his life.

Saigyō's sadness over the collapse of the society he had known is best understood by recalling its earlier magnificence. "Society" then meant one thing: the capital, called Heian. Known today as Kyoto, the city was founded in 794 after the ruling elite of Japan had for a long time failed in its attempts to establish a capital it could think of as "permanent." With a bureaucracy expanding in imitation of the Chinese system of government, there was a need for a settled place for palaces, offices, and rites. The site, therefore, was chosen with great care, and the city was named Heian-kyō or the "Peace-and-Tranquility Capital"—obviously with the hope that its conditions would live up to its name and, consequently, allow it to endure forever. Until the middle of the twelfth century, that is, for a period of almost three hundred and fifty years, it did prove to be a remarkably peaceful city. Some scholars see it as the most civilized society in the world at that time.

Poetry during this era was the badge of the cultivated life. It was, for the highly privileged minority, the principal medium of interpersonal communication—a fact fully reflected in the *Tale of Genji*, which Lady Murasaki wrote in the middle of the period. Through poetry people thanked the gods, celebrated the recurring festivals of each year, courted a mate or lover, lionized persons appointed to new posts, and added verbal ornament to excursions into the countryside. On those occasions when there was no "occasion" to celebrate, they simply marked the passage of time with lines to fit the season. But poetry was also linked to prestige. How well one performed at the often very competitive poetry contests always had a bearing on reputation and sometimes even on official rank. One man named Sanekata got so embroiled in an argument over poetry that he knocked off the status-marking cap of his adversary, a *faux pas* which, we are told, led to his exile from the capital. Poetry may have been play but, precisely because language is linked to power, it was also a very serious business in Heian-kyō.

Nature, too, was woven right into the fabric of everyday life. With forms of architecture so flexible that the distinction between indoors and outdoors often seemed imprecise, the citizens of Heian-kyō passed their days intimate with every nuance of seasonal change. The opening of certain blossoms, the encirclement by certain types of mist, the flights of certain birds, the sound of certain insects—all these became precise indexes to the passage of the year to a people with the leisure to observe and write about just when and how such things take place. Great wealth, too, was theirs, and it enabled these courtiers to decorate their clothing and their dwellings with the shapes and colors of natural things; gorgeously painted silk-screens and many-layered kimonos accommodated a wide variety of flowers, birds, and other things. But the attention to nature, of course, involves a certain selection, and it is clear that the elite of Heian-kyō preferred to notice and relish what was gentle and without the hint of physical threat. Steep precipices, deep and awesome forests, the turbulence of swollen rivers—these were all aspects of nature which these courtiers seemed not to have seen, or at least not to have put into their poems. Theirs was a genteel taste, limited to what in nature was predictably benign—perhaps a reflection of their hope that the passage of time would treat them, the class of the privileged, gently.

The Buddhism that was the main intellectual and religious nourishment of the era was one which on the Asian continent had already developed a panoply of ceremonies and imagery neatly fitting what seems to have been the principal social demand placed upon religion in Heian-kyō. For these people had a strong stake in the persistence of the status quo. Buddhism lent them rites purportedly capable of keeping all threatening things at bay; it used language which reiterated the theme of "peace and tranquility" in hundreds of ways. But what is especially fascinating is that in Heian-kyō the traditionally central teaching of constant and unavoidable change—what in Japanese was called *mujō*—was given a "soft" interpretation. That is, although the doctrine of inescapable change had entered Japan from the continent, these courtiers chose not to see change as sudden, radical, or disruptive but, on the contrary, as something capable of being anticipated and therefore almost comfortable. They took the gentle, seasonal alterations within nature as the perfect paradigm for understanding *mujō*: change was what comes like the delicately falling cherry blossom or the exquisitely colored maple leaf. To their way of thinking, change was after all the mechanism which makes beauty possible. They did not think of it, or at least did not *wish* to think of it, as something that could come like a raging fire or an engulfing flood. These highly privileged courtiers placed the accent on change by rhythm, not by rupture.

We can often read the mind of an age in its principal metaphors, the history of which, according to George Steiner, we need as much as we need that of massacres. In the Heian period there was a rich development of the metaphor of botanical life, a metaphor that was always to have a certain fascination for the Japanese and one through which they have expressed much of their distinctive contribution to the world's artistic and intellectual history. The poetry and the titles given to poetry collections give abundant evidence of this. And so absorbed did people in this period become in the significance of vegetational life that monks debated at length whether or not plants and trees were sentient beings, the possessors of what they called "buddha-nature." At an imperially sponsored forensic match in 963 the scholar-monk Ryōgen argued that plants and trees were perfected Buddhist yogis who take their origin in the "seed of enlightenment," practice the path of austere discipline by remaining fixed and quiet in one spot, put forth the flower of attainment, and then pass away into nirvana without stress or strain. During the same century, with words that lent the metaphor to subsequent articulations of the Japanese aesthetic, Ki no Tsuruyuki in his preface to the first imperial collection of verse, the *Kokin-shū,* defined poetry as "seeds sown in the human heart and grown out into the countless form of countless words, the leaves of things."

But whatever might be the reasons for the persistence of this metaphor in Japanese history, the fact that it gave the elite of Heian-kyō a comfortable way to think about change cannot be denied. In their established position, they obviously wanted no social upheaval. Change, if it had to come, was something they wished to confine to small, slow, and gentle forms. For this type of change could be anticipated, watched, and even controlled. The botanical metaphor fit this requirement perfectly. The scattering of blossoms and the elegant fall of a maple leaf served as fit similes for the end of an affaire d'amour and even for the close of someone's life. Sadness was consoled by beauty, and in the background was the implicit notion of seasonal return, the thought that change is in a cycle and in this, at least, does not itself change. The Heian courtiers' stress on the homology between human events and the calm cadences in the botanical world seems itself to have been part of an invocation, the expression of the hope that change would never prove to be other than benign. It was language intended to perform the magic of keeping what Mircea Eliade has called the "terror of history" at bay.

But it did not work. Already in the eleventh century, but much more obviously by the middle of the twelfth, a critical change appeared in the pattern of change itself. The rhythms of reality no longer seemed to be steady and predictable. The jockeying for positions of political power became rough, and even the monastic institutions were antagonistic to one another. From the last decade of the eleventh century onward it quite frequently happened that armed monks or their hired mercenaries attacked and burned rival temples. Military force became the tactic of the times. Then in 1156 an attempted coup d'etat spilled blood in the streets of the Peace-and-Tranquility Capital, and fifty of its supporters were put to death. Capital punishment, which for three hundred and fifty years had not been applied to crimes committed by courtiers, was reintroduced and administered with what seemed to be a vengeance. Most serious of all, however, was the struggle between two great clans with vast wealth and strong roots in the provinces, the Taira and the Minamoto, which went on for decades until the latter decisively grasped the power in 1185. The actual seat of government was then moved east to the still rustic frontier town of Kamakura. The glorious period called the Heian was clearly at an end. The kind of "history" the courtiers had wanted never to see, the type that brings rude and radical change, had come to the capital at last.

With this came a development in the language used to depict *mujō,* the Buddhist teaching about change. The docile botanical metaphor, which for so long had seemed to work so well, now yielded to geometeorological ones—at least for a while. Tapping the ancient Chinese belief that political disruptions go together with upheavals in the earth and destructive forms of weather, the history books at the end of the Heian period began to take increasing note of floods, fires, and earthquakes. By the time that Kamo no Chōmei wrote his celebrated *Account of My Hut* in 1212 the concept of *mujō* had been deepened and given a "hard" interpretation: change comes like wars, like earthquakes, and like floods, bringing sudden ruin to great houses and devastation even to cities thought eternal. The understanding of Buddhism had itself undergone a change, and even the idea of what was included within "nature" had been extended. Therefore, poetry too—its range of subjects, its perceptual field, its allowable diction—would also have to expand.

Saigyō was the poet at this pivot of change, the one in whose verse the whole process is most clearly seen. But charting his life is less easy. Although he left detailed information about some aspects of it, he seems deliberately to have left other parts in mystery. The medieval legends, which attempted to fill in what he had left obscure, are of no direct help. Our reliable data come from a few contemporaneous sources and from the notes he affixed to his own poems. The basics of these will be sketched here.

A reliable genealogical record tells us that he was born into the Satō sub-branch of the vast and powerful Fujiwara clan; his given name was Norikiyo. It was a military family with a reputation for valor and, at least initially, Norikiyo followed this tradition by becoming a captain in an elite corps of guards who protected the imperial family and the highest courtiers. He was taken into the Tokudaiji household, the two principal male members of which served at one time or another as the very highest ministers of state.

This household was one frequented by the very best poets of the age. The site of poetry contests, it was certainly the place where the young Norikiyo could sharpen his own skills at verse. Nevertheless, at this point he was noticed more for his horsemanship, swordsmanship, and ability in kick-ball than he was for verse. From one poem he was asked to contribute on a certain social occasion (p. 23) we can sense that, although he was physically close to the courtiers, it was as their guard rather than their social equal. It is also likely that in this same household he first witnessed aspects of the more seamy underside of Heian society. Years before, a daughter of the Tokudaiji family had become the consort of Emperor Toba and had given birth to a child who, in turn, himself became an emperor, Sutoku. But rumor had it that this child had been fathered not by Toba but by Toba's own grandfather, the Retired Emperor Shirakawa. In time this led to a legitimacy and succession struggle that shook the household, most likely becoming serious precisely during the years Norikiyo lived in its midst. The attempted coup d'etat in 1156 was, at least in part, a result of these events. Although by that time Norikiyo had become a monk, it is clear not only that he had known the people involved in these events but that he now lamented what was happening to them; his personal reaction is evident from the poems he wrote for them (pp. 39, 40, 57, 58).

The tense atmosphere of the household may have had quite a bit to do with his decision to become a Buddhist monk. Quite suddenly at the age of twenty-three he asked the emperor for permission to leave his commission (p. 84), although there is evidence that he had been thinking about such a move earlier (p. 34). His immediate reason for this break with secular life is nowhere given; both the medieval hagiographies and modern scholars have worked up a variety of explanations, but the truth is that nothing is known with any certainty. His exact motives remain a mystery. In fact, we do not even know whether at the time he had a wife—although the genealogy suggests that he had a son. He gave up his secular name, Norikiyo, and tried a couple of Buddhist names before settling on Saigyō, which means "West-Go" and serves as the one by which he has since been called. At first he lived on the outskirts of the capital, apparently in a private hermitage rather than in a temple or monastery.

Even before becoming a monk Saigyō had shown a certain fondness for placing himself in probative situations in which strength and endurance could be tested ("Taking off from Fushimi," p. 65). Now as a religious, this tendency continued and gained new importance—with periods of intentional self-deprivation, three extended pilgrimages into very remote areas, along with many shorter journeys, and the selection of lonely sites in the mountains for the practice of Buddhist austerities. The poetry gives candid portrayals of the continuing agon between that part of Saigyō still very much tied to the world and the other which strived for detachment as well as new possibilities of vision and poetry. This intentional suffering was understood by him as a condition for certain investigations—of loneliness, of residual passions, of karmic connections, of responses to death, and of the deep nexus between man and nature.

The first of two journeys to the far north began in 1147. Along the way Saigyō stopped at the grave of Sanekata, the poet of the past who had been sent into exile for becoming embroiled in an argument at court. Saigyō's poem at this man's graveside (p. 41) is probably evidence of his own fear that he, too, was sinking too far below the level of public visibility. The next year he returned to the capital, and for the next eight years we have no specific information about him. Scholars surmise that he sometimes lived near the great monastery at Mt. Kōya and at other times at Mt. Yoshino, a place famous for its cherry blossoms that Saigyō designated as his "home." He probably spent a good deal of time going from one spot to another, and his support came either from temple stores or from kinsmen, many of whom were wealthy and widely scattered over the areas through which he traveled. One poem by him ("So, then," p. 90) appeared anonymously in the *Shika-shū*, an imperial anthology that came out in 1151. Its theme fits the fact that it appeared without his name; Saigyō was ruminating on the paradox of having thrown his "self" away.

In 1156 the above-mentioned insurrection took place in the capital. Though soon crushed it served as the fuse for the long and bitter civil wars that eventually brought the era to an end. As we have seen, some court figures known personally to Saigyō either died or were exiled, and he responded directly to these events. Nevertheless, he seems to have resisted the prevalent but facile rationale that dire things were happening because the world had entered an age in which the knowledge of Buddhist teaching was necessarily in eclipse (p. 45). Saigyō preferred to hold that human resources remained what they always had been but that his contemporaries ought to join him in jettisoning the fraudulent values of society (p. 40).

His next major pilgrimage was to the island of Shikoku. He went there in 1168 at the age of fifty-one, visiting the grave of the exiled Retired Emperor Sutoku (p. 59) and sites sacred to the memory of Kūkai, the Buddhist holy man of the past most admired by Saigyō (pp. 59, 61). Along the road by the sea he observed the lives of divers and fishermen and wrote poems about their activities (pp. 62, 63), something absolutely unthinkable for the poets of the court. Ivan Morris, in his *World of the Shining Prince,* states the general norm very well: "Heian literature, which gives us such a detailed and vivid picture of how the gentry lived, has hardly a word to say about the masses. . . ." Fisherfolk were pariahs even in the world of poetry in those days, and it is significant that Saigyō felt compassion for these men and women whose livelihood was such that they were forced to kill to live. His pity lies within his ambivalence, but it is clear also that he found something to admire in their physical skills and the courage they showed in diving. For Saigyō this was reason enough to break the court taboo and open the range of verse to such a subject.

When he returned to the capital the two powerful clans were locked in their struggle for control of the country; just then it was the Taira who had gained hegemony over the court. Saigyō's relations with this family seem to have been fairly close, and in 1172 he was invited by its head, Kiyomori, to write a celebratory verse for a Buddhist extravaganza being held to open a new port for trade with

Sung China (p. 42). It is a type of public and official verse rare in Saigyō's work, and banal at that. Much better are the poems he wrote and sent as greetings to other poets, many of whom were monks or nuns. From some of the poems of this period we detect that he was involved in an amorous relationship; erotic in intention and imagery, they are addressed to someone cryptically referred to as "some person."

In 1180 he moved to Ise (p. 86), the most sacred site of Shinto. This was the time when the most bitter and devastating battles between the Taira and Minamoto were being waged. That same year Kiyomori suddenly moved the entire government and imperial family out of Heian-kyō. Saigyō took note of this, writing a poem contrasting the vicissitudes of man's capital cities with the dependable clarity of the moon (p. 87). The tragedy of the war moved him deeply. In the note to one poem (p. 74) he reflects on the death and devastation and asks rhetorically: "And for what on earth was this struggle taking place?" But the conflict continued until 1185, when the commander of the Minamoto, Yoritomo, prevailed over the Taira and set up his government in the east, in Kamakura.

Saigyō now at the age of sixty-nine traveled again to the northeast, taking basically the same route he had followed thirty-nine years earlier. On the way he passed through Kamakura and had an occasion to meet Yoritomo, the man who had just become dictator through his victories. The *Azuma Kagami* ("Mirror of the East"), a historical record compiled in the following century, provides an account of the encounter between the old monk and the notoriously suspicious-minded Yoritomo.

Yoritomo happened to see an aged monk at the local shrine and inquiring who he was learned that it was an officer of the imperial guard now become a Buddhist monk. The dictator then invited Saigyō to visit him at his mansion. When Saigyō arrived, he was requested to discuss both "the way of poetry" and the arts of archery and horsemanship. To this the old man replied:

"As for skills with the bow and on horses, there was once a time—namely, when I was still in secular life—when I quite imperfectly worked on these and in such a way carried on the traditions of my family. But during the eighth month of the third year of the Hōen era I became disenchanted with life in society. When that happened, all those military skills which had been handed down to me—since I was the direct heir of Ason no Hidesato in the ninth generation—were destroyed and lost forever. Evil karma in my past led to this situation. Today in the deep parts of my soul nothing of these former things remains; all has gone into oblivion. As for the writing of poetry, that is nothing more than putting thirty-one syllables together when emotionally stirred by the sight of a flower or the moon. I know nothing of so-called 'depths' in the composition of verse. Since this is the situation, it would be out of place for me to want to say more about these things."

But the record goes on to say that Saigyō did, after all, talk right through the night with Yoritomo about archery and horsemanship. The next day the military man gave the monk a cat made of silver—which Saigyō promptly gave away to a child playing by the gate as he left. He was going north, it is said, to collect contributions for the rebuilding of the great temple, Tōdai-ji.

Some of the poems composed while on this journey (pp. 88, for example) are among Saigyō's best. There is now in his verse a sense both of coming death and the surprise of continued life, a wonder and a composure. After his return he sent a number of his poems to other poets for their judgment and put together the verses that in their collected form he would call the *Sanka-shū* or "Mountain-Home-Collection." A rather remarkable poem he composed some time earlier in his life was the one in which he vowed to die during the full-moon period of the second lunar month, traditionally in Japan taken to be the anniversary of Sakyamuni's departure from this life (p. 7). When in the spring of 1190 Saigyō died precisely as he had said, the poem was viewed by his contemporaries as predictive in a preternatural way, securing his reputation as a Buddhist saint and spawning the medieval hagiographies about him. But his verse, too, now came to be widely recognized as a remarkable achievement, and in the next major imperial anthology, the *Shinkokin-shū*, Saigyō's poems outnumbered those of any other poet.

There is in Saigyō's reaction to his times and in his sense of suffering in solitude something which might seem to resemble the *Weltschmerz* and self-pity of certain poets in the Romantic tradition of the West. Nevertheless, there is a decisive difference, one which stems apparently from Saigyō's agreement with the traditional Buddhist claim that the ego-elevated perspective distorts reality and leaves too many important and beautiful phenomena below the level of vision. What Saigyō's verse celebrates, first of all, is not the self that sees but the phenomena which are seen. More accurately, we might say that the phenomenon and the self are both equally elevated when not in competition or contention. Saigyō's vision derives in part from Japanese Shinto's traditional reverence for nature, but it also is a part of that largesse in Mahayana Buddhism which earlier had led a monk such as Ryōgen to argue that plants and trees too are Buddhist yogis, participants with man in Buddhahood. Saigyō's diction captured it simply; to a degree unusual for poetry of that time he addressed the various phenomena of nature simply as "tomo" or companion (pp. 3, 27, 48). The mental posture in the poems is clear and expresses in concrete form something of what Buddhists call "codependent origination" or the fact that in no thing is there a trace of that being's having its existence in and of itself alone. All things are fully interdependent. "Depth" in nature, then, was not a Platonic realm of being somewhere behind concrete phenomena but a discoverable play of free interrelatedness. Saigyō found this play best expressed in nature; it was what man would do well to mirror in his own existence. It is a "satori" or enlightenment patent in the opened blossom and the clarity of the moon (p. 69).

And here, probably, is the subtle nexus between this vision of the ego-free interdependence in nature and the view of society which Saigyō felt compelled to take. For in his day the realm of man seemed to have lost the secret still retained by nature; inflated, exaggerated, and basically fictive "selves" were bent, sometimes with whole armies behind them, against one another and against the common good. Neither courtiers in the capital (pp. 20, 89) nor monks in their monasteries (p. 63) seemed able any longer to comprehend the mutuality and depth nature provided. Saigyō apparently conceived of his own agon as what was necessary to discover an alternative to society's agony. Resolution of the problem of the "self" was fundamental.

As a result the "nature" admitted into his poetry no longer needed to be limited to what was acceptable to a society repressing all but what was benign and comforting. The delicate flowers and garden butterflies remain in Saigyō's diction; but they are complemented by penetrating rains, steep ascents, and jabbering monkeys. Nature need not be always soft. And in line with this the sensibility of the poet opened in order to admit the beauty of the bleak and colorless (pp. 15, 24, 49)—in ways often associated with the monochromes of Zen painting. Winter, like loneliness and like death, has its place in the economy of coexistent things. The result was what Bashō found in Saigyō, "a mind both obeying and at one with nature throughout the four seasons."

Kenneth Rexroth in the introduction to his *One Hundred Poems from the Japanese* and Earl Miner in *An Introduction to Japanese Court Poetry* tell us all that is important about how a waka works as verse, while *Japanese Court Poetry* by Robert Brower and Earl Miner traces in detail the history of this verse form. I have nothing to add—except to note that Saigyō sometimes suspended syntax so that the whole might come together in an illuminative way at the end; something of this intentional strangeness is retained in the English here. But overall I have tried to keep the music that readers of Saigyō find in his poems. And I have tried to be "economical" in the best sense, that is, by neither overestimating nor underestimating the amount of words necessary to make the carry-over from one language to another. Terseness is a value in waka but should not, I think, lead one to skimp on the richness of nuance, affect, and association.

Translators, too, find that what they do is a process—perhaps even a path. There are lots of places along the way that deserve remembering. I owe much to people who, in various stages, read Saigyō or these translations with me. Norma, my best critic, was also always my best support. Professors Joseph M. Kitagawa and Masamichi Kitayama insisted I look for what is religious in Saigyō's poetry and for what was poetic in his religion. In addition, I profited especially from readings with Gary Snyder, the poets of *Kuksu*, Michael McClure, Jim Brazell, John Peck, and Yasuko Shimizu. My colleague Earl Miner provided invaluable comments. Freda Murck graciously helped me locate the cover painting of Saigyō in the Powers Collection.

WILLIAM R. LaFleur

MIRROR FOR THE MOON

toshi kurenu	Closed out the old year
haru kubeshi to wa	And held a dream of spring behind
omoine ni	My shut eyes . . . til now
masashiku miete	This morning I open them to see
kanau hatsuyume	It's really come into the world.

Celebrating spring at each house:

kado goto ni	Gate after gate
tatsuru komatsu ni	Adorned with festal pine:
kazasarete	Spring has come
yado chō yado ni	To each and every house
haru wa kinikeri	Garnishing all with new green.

haru shire to	Waking me up
tani no hosomizu	To the spring that's come,
mori zo kuru	Water trickles down
iwama no kōri	The valley and long crag-bound ice
hima taenikeri	Now cracks open, slides free.

At the place called Futami ["Two-Views"] in Ise:

nami kosu to
Futami no matsu no
mietsuru wa
kozue ni kakaru
kasumi narikeri

Look at it one way
And high waves seem to engulf
The pines at Futami
But then . . . again . . . you see
Mist masking the treetops.

haru no hodo wa
waga sumu io no
tomo ni narite
furusu na ide so
tani no uguisu

Spanning all of spring
As companion for me, an other
In a hermit's hut—
Don't forsake your nest
Here in the valley, warbler!

kumo nakute	Clouds dispersed
oboro nari to mo	And still it looks vague,
miyuru kana	Dreamy up there:
kasumi kakareru	Tonight's moon hanging
haru no yo no tsuki	In the haze of spring.

yamagatsu no	Penniless woodcutter
kataoka kakete	Managed to get for himself a hut
shimuru io no	Hanging on a steep slope
sakai ni tateru	And as boundary mark a gem,
tama no oyanagi	A jade-green young willow tree.

Yoshino yama	Journeying alone:
kozue no hana o	Now my body knows the absence
mishi hi yori	Even of its own heart,
kokoro wa mi ni mo	Which stayed behind that day when
sowazunariniki	It saw Yoshino's treetops.

hikikaete	In spring I spend day
hana miru haru wa	With flowers, wanting no night;
yoru wa naku	It's turned around
tsuki miru aki wa	In fall when I watch the moon
niru nakaranan	All night, resenting the day.

hana chirade   A world without
tsuki wa kumoran   The scattering of blossoms,
  yo nariseba   Without the clouding
mono o omowan   Over of the moon would deprive
waga mi naramashi   Me of my melancholy.

hana ni somu   Why do I, who broke
kokoro wa ikade   So completely with this world,
  nokoriken   Find in my body
sutehateteki to   Still the pulsing of a heart
omou waga mi ni   Once dyed in blossoms' hues?

    negawaku wa   Let it be this way:
hana no shita nite Under the cherry blossoms,
    haru shinan   A spring death,
sono kisaragi no   At that second month's midpoint
mochizuki no koro When the moon is full.

    hotoke ni wa   When gone in death,
sakura no hana o   I'll have cherry blossoms
    tatematsure   As your rite for me . . .
waga nochi no yo o If any wishes to make memorial here
hito toburawaba   For me in my life over there.

On seeing an ancient cherry tree with blossoms here and there:

wakite min	I must strain to see
oigi wa hana mo	The few buds this old tree
aware nari	Labored to open . . .
ima ikutabi ka	In pathos we're one and I wonder
haru ni aubeki	How many more springs we'll meet here.

When the blossoms were out at Mountain Temple; Recollections of long ago:

Yoshino yama	I found my way up
hokiji tsutai ni	Yoshino's precipice-hung
tazuneirite	Path and into its
hana mishi haru wa	Past, seeing there the blossoms
hito mukashi kamo	I sought that spring—ages ago.

While undertaking religious disciplines, I was in a place which had attractive blossoms:

   nagamuru ni   If my rapt gaze
hana no nadate no   Would not give rise to rumor
   mi narazu ba   And disgrace, I'd
kono moto nite ya   Want to spend all spring fixed here,
haru o kurasan   Feasting my eyes on these flowers.

Having withdrawn from the world, I was on the hills called Higashiyama and, at someone's invitation, went to see blossoms at Shirakawa; but I soon left and returned, reflecting on the past like this:

   chiru o mide   This frame of mind
kaeru kokoro ya   Lets me go back even without
   sakurabana   Seeing the blossoms fall:
mukashi ni kawaru Maybe it's some sign I am
shirushi naruran   No more the one I used to be.

nagamu tote
hana ni mo itaku
narenureba
chiru wakere koso
kanashi kari kere

"Detached" observer
Of blossoms finds himself in time
   Intimate with them—
So, when they separate from the branch,
It's he who falls . . . deeply into grief.

ko no moto ni
tabine o sureba
Yoshino yama
hana no fusuma o
kisuru harukaze

Tired from travel,
I'm falling asleep under
   A tree at Yoshino
While a spring breeze gathers
And pulls over me a quilt of petals.

        kaze sasou   Seduced by the warm breeze,
   hana no yukue wa   My blossoms went off with it
        shiranedomo   To who-knows-where;
   oshimu kokoro wa   So, loath to lose them, my heart
   mi ni tomarikeri   Stays here with nothing but my own self.

        harukaze no   In my dream I saw
   hana o chirasu to   The spring wind gently shaking
        miru yume wa   Blossoms from a tree;
   sametemo mune no   And even now, though I'm awake,
   sawagu nari keri   There's motion, trembling in my chest.

iwa tsutai	Scaling the crags
orade tsutsuji o	Where azalea bloom . . . not for plucking
te ni zo toru	But for hanging on!
sakashiki yama no	The saving feature of this rugged
toridokoro ni wa	Mountain face I'm climbing.

samidare no	Early summer rains:
harema mo mienu	No let-up, no glimpse of sky,
kumoji yori	But somewhere inside
yama hototogisu	This thick bank of clouds a crying
nakite sugunari	Mountain warbler threads its ways.

Finding a cool place in summer at North Shirakawa:

mizu no oto ni
atsusa wasururu
matoi kana
kozue no semi no
koe mo magirete

Next to murmuring waters
We're a circle of friends, no longer
   Minding summer's heat,
And the cicada voices in the treetops
Mix in well with all the rest.

obotsukana
aki wa ikanaru
yue no areba
suzuro ni mono no
kanashikaruran

All so vague:
In autumn the reasons why
   All fall away
And there's just this
Inexplicable sadness.

Under the moon, looking far into the distance:

kuma mo naki
tsuki no hikari ni
sasowarete
iku kumoi made
yuku kokoro zo mo

So taken with
The faultless face and radiance
Of an alluring moon,
My mind goes farther . . . farther . . .
To reach remote regions of the sky.

oi mo senu
jūgo no toshi mo
aru mono o
koyoi no tsuki no
kakaramashikaba

To be just fifteen!
A time without infirmities,
The moon's age tonight,
As full in the midst of its life
It is suspended, perfect now.

mushi no ne ni	Insect cries more faint
kareyuku nobe no	In these clumps of autumn grass
kusamura ni	Going dry: sympathy
aware o soete	Lent this field by shafts
sumeru tsukikage	Of the moon's light on it.

ko no ma moru	Tree-filtered
ariake no tsuki o	Patch of moonlight fades with dawn;
nagamureba	Staring at it gives
sabishisa souru	Loneliness . . . deepened by winds
mine no matsukaze	Soughing through pines on the peaks.

abaretaru	This leaky, tumbledown
kusa no iori ni	Grass hut left opening for the moon,
moru tsuki o	And I gazed at it
sode ni utsushite	All the while it was mirrored
nagametsuru kana	In a teardrop fallen on my sleeve.

yukue naku	Limitations gone:
tsuki ni kokoro no	Since my mind fixed on the moon,
sumi sumite	Clarity and serenity
hate wa ika ni ka	Make something for which
naran to suran	There's no end in sight.

kumo haruru
arashi no oto wa
　matsu ni are ya
tsuki mo midori no
iro ni haetsutsu

The clouds dissolved
But the storm's sound still lingers on
　In swishing pine boughs—
Maybe why some of the trees' blue
Tints the moon up there now.

kuma mo naki
tsuki no omote ni
　tobu kari no
kage o kumo ka to
magaetsuru kana

Not a hint of shadow
On the moon's face . . . but now
　A silhouette passes—
Not the cloud I take it for,
But a flock of flying geese.

moro tomo ni	Next to my own
kage o naraburu	It would be good to have
hito mo are ya	Another's shadow
tsuki no morikuru	Cast here in the pool of moonlight
sasa no io ni	Leaked into my hut of bamboo grass.

During a journey; concerning the moon:

tsuki wa nao	As always, the moon
yo na yo na goto ni	Night after night after night
yadorubeshi	Will stay on here
waga musubioku	At this grass hut I put together—
kusa no iori ni	And now myself must leave.

With my mind made up to go to worship at Aki Shrine, I was in a place called Takatomi Cove, where I waited for a gale to subside. The moon filtered through the reed roof of my hut:

nami no oto o   Pounding waves are breakers . . .
kokoro ni kakete   Of my heart, so I spend the night
   akasu kana   In bed with the moon's
toma moru tsuki no   Light that slips in through
kage o tomo nite   The gaps in my reed hut's roof.

Setting out on a pilgrimage and feeling profound sentiments with respect to an especially bright moon:

moro tomo ni   We would together
tabi naru sora ni   Make the journey, I on land
   tsuki idete   And it in the sky,
sumebaya kage no   If the moon comes out to stay:
aware naruran   Empathy both ways.

miyako nite	Back in the capital
tsuki o aware to	We gazed at the moon, calling
omoishi wa	Our feelings "deep"—
kazu yori hoka no	Mere shallow diversions
susabi narikeri	That here don't count at all.

Morning; hearing the first geese:

yokogumo no	Pushed along by wind,
kaze ni wakaruru	Clouds layered along the peaks
shinonome ni	Diffuse at daybreak:
yama tobikoyuru	Honking geese who've crossed
hatsu kari no koe	The mountains open the fall.

The voices of geese—far and near:

shirakumo o   Wings already wet
tsubasa ni kakete   By the cold clouds he's entered,
   yuku kari no   A gander calls out
kadota no omo no   Yearning for his mate who sits here
tomo shitau nari   In the field just outside the gate.

nagori ōki   Lovers' rendezvous
mutsugoto tsukide   Slowly ends with many vows
   kaeriyuku   To let nothing come
hito o ba kiri mo   Between them . . . then, as he moves off,
tachihedatekeri   Rising mists hide him from her.

At a quiet place away from it all; on hearing a deer:

tonari inu　　　　None other is anywhere
hara no kariya ni　Near this borrowed field shed,
akasu yo wa　　　　So the crying til
shika aware naru　Daybreak must be a deer's:
mono ni zo arikeru　Alone with all other things.

A ricefield, a hermitage, and a deer:

oyamada no　　　　Quiet mountain hut
io chikaku naku　By a rice patch . . . til a deer's cry
shika no ne ni　　Just outside startles me
odorokasarete　　And I move . . . so startling him:
odorokasu kana　　We astonish one another!

While Fujiwara Munesuke was middle counselor, he presented a large number of chrysanthemums as a gift to Retired Emperor Toba. When planted, they filled the area of the eastern garden of Toba's southern palace. Kimishige, who [later] was to be a captain of the imperial guard, invited a number of people to write verses celebrating these chrysanthemums, and I was pleased to be included among those asked to do so:

kimi ga sumu
yado no tsubo o ba
   kiku zo kazaru
hijiri no miya to
iubekaruran

Chrysanthemums fill
The garden where the days are passed
   By Your Majesty—
So "Grotto of the Holy Sage,"
The palace name, fits very well.

kokoro naki Thought I was free
mi ni mo aware wa Of passions, so this melancholy
shirarekeri Comes as surprise:
shigi tatsu sawa no A woodcock shoots up from marsh
aki no yūgure Where autumn's twilight falls.

michi mo nashi All roads disappeared
yado wa no-no-ha ni Under thickly fallen leaves,
uzumorete Which buried my place—
madaki sesasuru Completely out of season,
fuyugomori kana Locked in for winter already!

sabishisa ni	Someone who has learned
taetaru hito no	How to manage life in loneliness:
mata mo are na	Would there were one more!
iori naraben	He could winter here on this mountain
fuyu no yamazato	With his hut right next to mine.

fuyugare no	Winter has withered
susamajigenaru	Everything in this mountain place:
yamazato ni	Dignity is in
tsuki no sumu koso	Its desolation now, and beauty
aware narikere	In the cold clarity of its moon.

Arachi yama
sakashiku kudaru
tani mo naku
kajiki no michi o
tsukuru shirayuki

So steep and dangerous
Is Mount Arachi that there's
    No way down the valley . . .
Til one is made for snowshoes
By white snow fallen over all.

furu yuki ni
shiorishi shiba mo
uzumorete
omowan yama ni
fuyugomorinuru

When the fallen snow
Buried the twigs bent by me
    To mark a return trail,
Unplanned, in strange mountains
I was holed up all winter.

yuki fureba　　　　　Snow has fallen on
noji mo yamaji mo　　Field paths and mountain paths,
　uzumorete　　　　　　Burying them all
ochikochi shiranu　　And I can't tell here from there:
tabi no sora kana　　My journey in the midst of sky.

hitori sumu　　　　　Here I huddle, alone,
katayama kage no　　In the mountain's shadow, needing
　tomo nare ya　　　　　Some companion somehow:
arashi ni haruru　　The cold, biting rains pass off
fuyu no yo no tsuki　And give me the winter moon.

Having made my escape from a worldly way of life, I was in the interior of Kurama and at a bamboo conduit, the water of which was frozen and not running. Hearing from someone that this would be the situation until the arrival of spring, I wrote this poem:

warinashiya   It was bound to be:
kōru kakei no   My vow to be unattached
mizu yue ni   To seasons and such . . .
omoisuteteshi   I, who by a frozen bamboo pipe
haru no mataruru   Now watch and wait for spring.

Gone far to the northeast; at year's end:

tsune yori mo   A forlorn feeling
kokorobosoku zo   This time more sharp than ever:
    omōyuru   Journeying along
tabi no sora nite   Under a vast sky where I see
toshi no kurenuru   The old year sink to its close.

Passion for a blossom which still is not fallen:

hagakure ni   Hidden away
chiritodomareru   Under leaves, a blossom
    hana nomi zo   Still left over
shinobishi hito ni   Makes me yearn to chance upon
au kokochi suru   My secret love this way.

Love like cut reeds:

    hitokata ni   Not so confused
midaru to mo naki   As to lean only one way:
    waga koi ya   My love-life!
kaze sadamaranu   A sheaf of field reeds also bends
nobe no karu kaya   Before each wind which moves it.

Love like fallen leaves:

    asa goto ni   Each morning the wind
koe o osamuru   Dies down and the rustling leaves
    kaze no oto wa   Go silent: Was this
yo o hete karuru   The passion of all-night lovers
hito no kokoro ka   Now talked out and parting?

omokage no
wasurarumajiki
wakare kana
nagori o hito no
tsuki ni todomete

I'll never forget
Her look when I said goodbye . . .
Especially since,
As keepsake, she set her sorrow-
Filled face on the moon above.

yoshi saraba
namida no ike ni
mi o nashite
kokoro no mama ni
tsuki o yadosan

It will be good:
My body may cry itself into
A pond of tears,
But in it my unchanged heart
Will give lodging to the moon.

omokage ni
kimi ga sugata o
　mitsuru yori
niwaka ni tsuki no
kumorinuru kana

In the portrait
Emerging on the moon I spied
　Your face . . . so clearly,
The cause of tears which then
Quickly cast the moon in clouds again.

kuma mo naki
ori shi mo hito o
　omoidete
kokoro to tsuki o
yatsushitsuru kana

No pock nor shadow
On the moon's face, so just then
　I recalled yours—clear
Til tears from my own mind
Defaced the moon once more.

tsukuzuku to　　　　In deep reverie
mono o omoi ni　　On how time buffets all,
uchisoete　　　　　I hear blows fall
ori aware naru　　On a temple bell . . . drawing out more
kane no oto kana　Of its sounds and my sadness.

noki chikaki　　　　My kimono sleeves,
hana tachibana ni　Blossom-scented by the air
sode shimete　　　　Under this orange tree
mukashi o shinobu　Close by the eaves, catch and hold
namida tsutsuman　Tears falling from the past's recall.

During the time I was coming to a decision about leaving secular life, I was on Higashiyama with a number of people and we were composing verses expressing what we felt about gathering mists there:

sora ni naru
kokoro wa haru no
kasumi nite
yo ni araji tomo
omoitatsu kana

A man whose mind is
At one with the sky-void steps
    Inside a spring mist
And thinks to himself he might
In fact step right out of the world.

fukaki yama wa
hito mo toikonu
sumai naru ni
obitadashiki wa
mura zaru no koe

Here I've a place
So remote, so mountain-closed,
    None comes to call.
But those voices! A whole clan
Of monkeys on the way here!

While secluded in a place far away, the moon conveyed my message all the way back to someone in the capital:

tsuki nomi ya	The moon, like you,
ue no sora naru	Is far away from me, but it's
katami nite	Our sole memento:
omoi mo ideba	If you look and recall our past
kokoro kayowan	Through it, we now can be one mind.

Having left the world, I was at Suzukayama ["Deer-bell Mountain"] on the way to Ise:

Suzukayama	On Deer-bell Mountain!
uki yo o yoso ni	My being here means I pushed away
furisutete	The swaying world now;
ika ni nariyuku	But what's to be my life's timbre
waga mi naruran	Can't be heard in this bell's murmur.

nanigoto ni
tomaru kokoro no
    arikereba
sara ni shi mo mata
yo no itowashiki

When, at this stage
Of world-loathing, something captures
    The heart, then indeed
The same world is all the more
Worthy . . . of total disdain.

toshitsuki o
ikade waga mi ni
    okuriken
kinō no hito mo
kyō wa naki yo ni

Why, in this world where
One here yesterday is off today
    To the world of death,
Are more and more years and still
More and more months given me?

On the way to the temple called Tennō-ji, I got caught in the rain. In the area known as Eguchi I asked at one place for a night's lodging. When refused, I replied as follows:

yo no naka o
itou made koso
    katakarame
kari no yadori o
oshimu kimi kana

It is hard, perhaps,
To hate and part with the world;
    But you are stingy
Even with the night I ask of you,
A place in your soon-left inn.

The response by a "woman of pleasure":

ie o izuru
hito to shi kikeba
    kari no yado ni
kokoro tomuna to
omou bakari zo

It's because I heard
You're no longer bound to life
    As a householder
That I'm loath to let you get attached
To this inn of brief, bought, stays.

Under the moon, recollecting the past:

tsuki o mite   That moon up there:
izure no toshi no   How many more autumns will
    aki made ka   I be here to see it?
kono yo ni ware ga   Something long ago fixed for
chigiri aruran   This life by an earlier one.

At a point in time when I was feeling desolate, I heard the voice of a
cricket very close to my pillow:

sono ori no   At that turning point
yomogi ga moto no   With my head for the last time
    makura ni mo   Pillowed in sagebrush,
kaku koso mushi no   I'd have this chirping insect
ne ni wa mutsureme   Still be what's closest to me.

My fellow-pilgrim [the monk Saijū] had an illness which had reached the critical point; under a bright moon, my sadness:

morotomo ni   Side by side, year
nagame nagamete   After year, you and I
aki no tsuki   Gazed and gazed
hitori ni naran   At the autumn moon, which now
koto zo kanashiki   Seen alone is the sum of sadness.

On the occasion when the remains of Retired Emperor Toba were being carried to the place of entombment:

michi kawaru   Different from places
miyuki kanashiki   Your Majesty visited before!
koyoi kana   Tonight's sad, final
kagiri no tabi to   Journey in this world takes you
miru ni tsuketemo   Far beyond the world itself.

During the period of mourning for his father, Tokudaiji Kin 'yoshi's mother died as well. Having heard of this, I sent the following in condolence to him from Mount Kōya:

kasane kiru	One on another . . .
fuji no koromo o	Wisteria robes of mourning
tayori nite	Ever deeper—
kokoro no iro o	Suggest you might now dye
someyo to zo omou	Your life in the Dharma's depth.

Tokudaiji Kin 'yoshi's response:

fujigoromo	The color of my
kasanuru iro wa	Body garments may have deepened
fukakeredo	But my mind
asaki kokoro no	Is still shallow, pale,
shimanu hakanasa	Unfit for such a step.

While in the province of Mutsu I came across an unusual looking grave mound. I asked someone whose it was and was told that it belonged to a middle captain of the palace guards. When I persisted in inquiring about just who this captain might have been, I was informed that it was Fujiwara Sanekata—and I was very saddened. Even before learning these details, I had sensed the pathos in this scene of frost-shriveled pampas grass, so faint it was almost invisible. Later, trying to express what I felt, words too were almost nonexistent:

kuchi mo senu	One part of him
sono na bakari o	Escaped decay, his name,
todomeokite	Still around here like
kareno no susuki	This bleak field's withered grass:
katami ni zo miru	My view of the relic he left.

shi nite fusamu
koke no mushiro o
omou yori
kanete shiraruru
iwakage no tsuyu

My cold corpse
Covered forever with moss
   For bedding will
Recollect what it learned here
From dew on a rock's cold, dark side.

Taira Kiyomori assembled a thousand Buddhists for a service of sutra recitations at the place called Wada in Tsu province. Later a special ceremony for the lighting of a myriad lanterns was held; as night deepened one could see the lamps go out and then, one by one, be relit:

kienubeki
nori no hikari no
tomoshibi o
kakaguru Wada no
tomari narikeri

The way of lamps
Is to flicker and die in time,
   But these of the Dharma
Shed light again here at Wada,
Anchorage in the night.

yamanoha ni
kakaruru tsuki o
  nagamureba
ware to kokoro no
nishi ni iru kana

Staring at the moon
As it dips down and hides itself
  On the mountain's other side,
I sense that my own mind goes
Willingly toward its own West.

yamakawa no
minagiru mizu no
  oto kikeba
semuru inochi zo
omoishiraruru

The sound of a swollen
Mountain stream rapidly rushing
  Makes one know
How very quickly life itself
Is pressed along its course.

ada naranu	Nothing lost . . .
yagate satori ni	Since in satori everything
kaerikeri	Thrown away
hito no tame ni mo	Comes back again: the life
sutsuru inochi wa	Given up for an "other."

madoikite	My dilemma:
satori ubeku mo	That deep realization will
nakaritsuru	Never come to
kokoro o shiru wa	My mind, the truth of which
kokoro narikeri	My mind realizes all too well.

yami harete	The mind is a sky
kokoro no sora ni	Emptied of all darkness,
sumu tsuki wa	And its moon,
nishi no yamabe ya	Limpid and perfect, moves
chikaku naruran	Closer to mountains in the West.

On that chapter of the *Lotus Sutra* called "Duration of the Life of the Tathagata":

Washi-no-yama	Those who view the moon
tsuki o irinu to	Over Vulture Peak as one
miru hito wa	Now sunk below
kuraki ni mayou	The horizon . . . are men whose minds,
kokoro nari keri	Confused, hold the real darkness.

no ni tateru
eda naki ko ni mo
　　otorikeri
nochi no yo shiranu
hito no kokoro wa

When a man gives no
Mind to what follows this life,
　　He's worse off than
That tree trunk standing in a field:
No branch or twig anywhere.

izuku ni ka
mi o kakusamashi
　　itoite mo
ukiyo ni fukaki
yama nakariseba

What a wretched world
This would be if this depised,
　　Quickly passing world
Had no place to hide away—
That is, no mountains in it.

asaku ideshi　　　The mind for truth
kokoro no mizu ya　Begins, like a stream, shallow
　tatauran　　　　At first, but then
sumiyuku mama ni　Adds more and more depth
fukaku naru kana　While gaining greater clarity.

tou hito mo　　　Hoped-for, looked-for
omoitaetaru　　　Guests just never made it to
　yamazato no　　My mountain hut—
sabishisa nakuba　The now congenial loneliness
sumiukaramashi　 I'd hate to live without.

    mizu no oto wa   The sound of water
sabishiki io no   Gets to be my sole comfort in
    tomo nare ya   This lonely, battered hut:
mine no arashi no   In the midst of mountain storm's fury
taema taema ni   Drops drip in the holes and silences.

    tazunekite   This place of mine
kototou hito no   Never is entered by humans
    naki yado ni   Come for conversation,
ko no ma no tsuki no   Only by the mute moon's light shafts
kage zo sashikuru   Which slip in between the trees.

aware ni zo
monomekashiku wa
    kikoekeru
karetaru nara no
shiba no ochiba wa

Patter of pathos:
A sound like falling hailstones,
    Awesome somehow:
Large leaves from the limbs
Of an old, now withered, oak.

furu hata no
soba no tatsu ki ni
    iru hato no
tomo yobu koe no
sugoki yūgure

Old field run to ruin
And in the sole tree starkly
    Rising on a bluff
Sits a dove, mourning its mate:
The awesome nightfall.

mase ni saku
hana ni mutsurete
tobu chō no
urayamashiku mo
hakanakari keri

Now seen . . . now gone,
The butterfly flits in and out
   Through fence-hung flowers;
But a life lived so close to them
I envy . . . though it's here and gone.

wabibito no
namida ni nitaru
sakura kana
kaze mi ni shimeba
mazu koboretsutsu

When stung by the world,
Man's tears spill drop by drop
   Like the cherry tree
Whose petals scatter down when
It is whipped by cold winds.

Yoshino yama　　　"He'll return," they think,
yagate ideji to　　"When the blossoms all are fallen,"
omou mi o　　　　　But he they wait for
hana chirinaba to　Himself is thinking now he'll
hito ya matsuran　　Never leave Mount Yoshino.

ware nare ya　　　　We're both afflicted
kaze o wazurau　　By drafts and wind, and spend our days
shinodake wa　　　　Getting up and lying down:
okifushi mono no　　Young bamboo with still-weak core
kokorobosokute　　And I, ill and disheartened.

After having been on a pilgrimage through many provinces, I was returning to Yoshino in the spring when someone asked me where I would be staying this time; I responded:

hana o mishi
mukashi no kokoro
   aratamete
Yoshino no sato ni
suman to zo omou

Returning to where
It used to see blossoms,
   My mind, changed,
Will stay on at Yoshino . . .
Home now, and see anew.

On seeing the moon at the place called Shinsen on Mount Ōmine:

fukaki yama ni
sumikeru tsuki o
   mizariseba
omoide mo naki
waga mi naramashi

Passage into dark
Mountains over which the moon
   Presides so brilliantly . . .
Not seeing it, I'd have missed
This passage into my own past.

tsuki sumeba	With the moon up there
tani ni zo kumo wa	So brilliant, all the clouds
shizumumeru	Sank low down
mine fukiharau	In the valley, urged along
kaze ni shikarete	By winds sweeping the peaks.

Stopping over at a place called Heichi, I saw the moon while it was reflected through the treetops and in drops on my sleeve:

kozue moru	Trickling in through
tsuki mo aware o	Tree foliage, the moon up there
omou beshi	Shows it knows
hikari ni gushite	Sadness: In its light here
tsuyu no koboruru	Lies the dew it wept tonight.

At a place called Ants' Crossing:

sasa fukami	Crack-of-morning
kiri kosu kuki o	Climb from caves in thick
asatachite	Bamboo grass beyond
nabiki wazurau	The mists: body now bending along
Ari-no-towatari	Stark rock forms at Ants' Crossing.

I visited someone who had renounced the world and now lives in Saga. We conversed about the importance for our future lives of daily and uninterrupted practice of our Buddhist faith now. Having returned, I took special notice of an upright shaft of bamboo and wrote this:

yoyo futomo	Linked worlds,
take no hashira no	Linked lives: on an
hitosuji ni	Upright shaft
tatetaru fushi wa	Of bamboo every joint
kawarazaranan	Is strong and straight.

Just as the beams of the sun were retreating before the night, those of the moon came in through my window:

sashikitsuru	The sun that shone
mado no irihi o	In my window now slipped
aratamete	Behind the horizon,
hikari o kauru	But suddenly light is renewed:
yūzukuyo kana	Shafts of the moon shine in.

On the [hanging] bridge near the Oku-no-In at Mount Kōya. The moon was unusually brilliant and I thought back to that time when the priest Saijū and I spent a whole night together viewing the moon from this same bridge. It was just before he left for the capital, and I will never forget the moon that night. Now that I am at exactly the same place, I wrote this for Saijū:

kototonaku	Somehow stretched
kimi koi wataru	From then to now is my love
hashi no ue ni	For you, held on this
arasou mono wa	Bridge of tension between tonight's
tsuki no kage nomi	Moon and the one I saw here with you.

yama fukami　　　　　Deep in the mountains,
koke no mushiro no　Sitting upright on moss used
　　ue ni ite　　　　　　　As a mat for himself
nani kokoro naku　　(With not a care in the world)
naku mashira kana　Is a gibbering, chattering ape.

yama fukami　　　　　Deep in the mountains,
kejikaki tori no　　　No call of any bird at all close
　　oto wa sede　　　　　And familiar . . .
mono osoroshiki　　Just the spine-tingling hoot
fukurō no koe　　　　Of that mountain owl.

A great calamity shook society, and things in the life of Retired Emperor Sutoku underwent inconceivable change, so that he took the tonsure and moved into the north quarters of the temple called Ninna-ji. I went there and met the eminent priest [Ācārya] Kengen. The moon was bright, and I composed the following verse:

kakaru yo ni   Times when unbroken
kage mo kawarazu   Gloom is over all our world . . .
sumu tsuki o   Over which still
miru waga mi sae   Sits the ever-brilliant moon:
urameshiki kana   Sight of it casts me down more.

After Retired Emperor Sutoku had gone to Sanuki and not much was heard in society about poetry any longer, I wrote the following to the priest Jakunen:

koto no ha no   Grievous fate: to find
nasake taetaru   You've come to be just at that
  orifushi ni   Juncture in time
ariau mi koso   When gatherings of refined poets
kanashikarikere   Are a custom just become . . . extinct.

au to mishi   That night when we met
sono yo no yume no   To make love in my dreams, I willed
  samede arena   To be a never
nagaki neburi wa   Awakened One . . . though it's said
ukarube keredo   Everlasting night is miserable fate.

Having come to Sanuki, I was at a place called the Cove of Matsuyama. I looked for the place where the retired emperor [Sutoku] had lived while [in exile] there, but no trace of his earlier presence could be found.

Matsuyama no
nami ni nagarete
koshi fune no
yagate munashiki
narinikeru kana

The ship he was on
Crossed the waves to Matsuyama
And then suddenly
Disappeared—as he too slipped
Down below our horizon.

I was in the province of Sanuki and in the mountains where Kōbō Daishi had lived; when there I stayed in a hut woven out of grasses. The moon was especially bright and, since the sky over the [Inland] Sea was cloudless, I could see it well:

kumori naki
yama nite umi no
tsuki mireba
shima zo kōri no
taema narikeru

Cloud-free mountains
Encircle the sea, which holds
The reflected moon:
A view of it there changes the islands
Into holes of emptiness in a sea of ice.

On seeing a tree which stood in front of my hermitage:

hisa ni hete
waga nochi no yo o
   toe yo matsu
ato shinobubeki
hito mo naki mi zo

Long-living pine,
Of you I ask: everlasting
   Mourning for me and
Cover for my corpse; here is no
Human to think of me when gone.

koto o mata
ware sumiukute
   ukarenaba
matsu wa hitori ni
naran to suran

If I settle here,
Pine, you'll be left again
   Alone when I
Tire of this place and
Wander off forever.

The climb up to Mandala Temple in order to perform the things a pilgrim does there was extraordinarily difficult. The climber must make an almost perpendicular ascent. It is a peak on which are buried Buddhist sutras which Kōbō Daishi [Kūkai] copied out with his own brush. Outside the priest's quarters [at the top] is a ten-foot-square dais. It is said that Kōbō Daishi climbed up on this place every day to perform religious observances. Now, so that others can do devotional activities there [without falling off], a double enclosure has been put around it. Still, the dangers faced in making the climb up to that spot are really unusual. I made my way up to the top by crawling on all fours.

meguriawan	Lucky to make it:
koto no chigiri zo	Here at this point where
arigataki	Holy ones met once
kibishiki yama no	To make pledges on abrupt
chikai miru ni mo	Precipices above it all.

When I crossed to the island known as Kojima in Bizen Province, I found myself in a place where people earned their living catching a tiny shrimp called the "ami." I saw that these fishermen attached a bag to a long pole and put this into the water. The first person to lift his shrimp-nabbing pole out of the water was called "first pole," and it was the most elderly fisherman among them who had the privilege of being called this. This [life-taking] activity is referred by them as the "lifting-up"—something that struck me [because we use the same word to refer to the "lifting up" of prayers and vows]. I was moved quite beyond my ability to express in words. I wept and then wrote this poem:

tatesomuru	Now lifting out
ami toru ura no	Of the bay a haul of shrimp
hatsusao wa	Is the first man's pole:
tsumi no naka ni mo	The looks of a superb catch
sururetaruran	Of sins . . . but also of fish.

I was at a place where I could see divers out in the open sea taking abalone from rocks under the water:

iwa no ne ni
kataomomuki ni
    namiukite
awabi o kazuku
ama no muragimi

Hanging on for life
To the rocks under them,
    Abalone watch
The master diver swimming
Down to pry them loose.

sutetaredo
kakurete sumanu
    hito ni nareba
nao yo ni aru ni
nitaru narikeri

To think you've
Thrown the world away and then
    Still live unhidden
Is to be like any other worldling
Still living in the world of men.

kuretake no	Lofty lord,
fushi shigekaranu	Like bamboo your world has
yo nariseba	Nodes, knuckles,
kono kimi wa tote	Complications one on another:
sashiidenamashi	If not so, I'd gladly serve in it.

se o hayami	Making my way
Miyataki-gawa o	Through the whirling rapids
watariyukeba	Of Miyataki River,
kokoro no soko no	I have the sense of being washed
sumu kokochi suru	Clean to the base of my heart.

nami to miyuru
yuki o wakete zo
   kogiwataru
Kiso no kakehashi
soko mo mieneba

   I push through snow
Like white surf on Kiso's
   Hanging bridge
(Gripping rails like oars):
Bottom too far below to see.

Fushimi suginu
Oka-no-ya ni nao
   todomaraji
Hino made yukite
koma kokoromin

   Taking off from Fushimi,
Galloping nonstop over
   Oka-no-ya's hills,
I'll spur him on to Hino
To test what this pony can do!

Yoshino yama
hana no chirinishi
ko no moto ni
tomeshi kokoro wa
ware o matsuran

Yoshino Mountains:
Blossoms tumbled to the foot
    Of trees, fastening
My heart there with them . . .
Waiting still for my return.

Yoshino yama
fumoto no taki ni
nagasu hana ya
mine ni tsumorishi
yuki no shitamizu

Yoshino Mountains:
Down here it is cascades of
    Water spread with
White petals; up there on the peaks
It starts out running under deep snow.

nanigoto ka
kono yo ni hetaru
　　omoide o
toekashi hito ni
tsuki o oshien

To that person
Wanting recall of events past
　　In this world below:
"Why not ask the moon above?"
May be the most fit response.

　kimi o ikade
komaka ni yueru
　　shigeme yui
tachi mo hararezu
narabitsutsu min

On you somehow
The close weave of that fine
　　Fabric will not come
Undone; would I were so close,
Myself interwoven with you.

sasagani no
ito ni tsuranuku
　tsuyu no tama o
kakete kazareru
yo ni koso arikere

Delicate dewdrops
On a spider's web are the pearls
　Strung on necklaces
Worn in the world man spins:
A world quickly vanishing.

utsutsu o mo
utsutsu to sara ni
　oboeneba
yume o mo yume to
nanika omowan

Since the "real world" seems
To be less than really real,
　Why need I suppose
The world of dreams is nothing
Other than a world of dreams?

yo no naka ni
nakunaru hito o
    kiku tabi ni
omoi wa shiru o
orokanaru mi ni

People pass away
And the truth of the passing world
    Impresses me
Now and then . . . but otherwise my dull
Wits let this truth too pass away.

On that chapter of the *Lotus Sutra* entitled "A Peaceful Life," and especially on the phrase "Entering deeply into meditation and seeing Buddhahood in all Ten Directions":

fukaki yama ni
kokoro no tsuki shi
    suminureba
kagami ni yomo no
satori o zo miru

In the mountains' deep
Places, the moon of the mind
    Resides in light serene:
Moon mirrors all things everywhere,
Mind mirrors moon . . . in satori now.

tomekokashi
ume sakari naru
　waga yado o
utoki mo hito wa
ori ni koso yore

Now's the time to visit!
Just when my place is full of
　Opened plum blossoms:
Long unseen humans too wait for
Just the right time to come forth.

hana no iro no
Yuki-no-miyama ni
　kayoeba ya
fukaki Yoshino no
oku e iraruru

Do the white blossoms
On my mountain take the place of
　Snow on the holy Himalayas?
I wish to enter the profound
Inner depths of Mount Yoshino.

fukenikeru　　　While noticing how time
waga mi no kage o　Has bent my body's silhouette
omou ma ni　　　　Cast in the moonlight . . .
haruka ni tsuki no　Away off in the distance the moon
katabukinikeru　　Sank closer to the world's rim.

haru goto no　　　Each and every spring
hana ni kokoro o　Blossoms gave my mind its
nagusamete　　　　Comfort and pleasure:
musoji amari no　　Now more than sixty years
toshi o henikeru　　Have gone by like this.

takeuma o
tsue ni mo kyō wa
    tanomu kana
warawaasobi o
omoiidetsutsu

Propped up by my cane,
I hobble along remembering
        My boyhood when
I loved the child's game of
Walking perched on bamboo stilts.

    omoiide ni
hana no nami ni mo
    nagareba ya
mine no shirakumo
taki kudasumeri

If only I could
Float along on a surf of blossoms
        I recall so well:
How they poured down from the heights
Like a cascade of white cloud.

Yoshino yama	Yoshino mountains—
oku o ware zo	The one who will get to know
shirinubeki	You inside-out is I,
hana yue fukaku	For I've gotten used to going
irinaraitsutsu	Into your depths for blossoms.

ukegataki	Rare achievement:
hito no sugata ni	This birth in a human form,
ukami idete	And so easily
korizu ya tare mo	Lost by not learning how
mata shizumuran	Not to sink below again.

In the world of men it came to be a time of warfare. Throughout the country—west, east, north, and south—there was no place where the war was not being fought. The count of those dying because of it climbed continually and reached an enormous number. It was beyond belief! And for what on earth was this struggle taking place? A most tragic state of affairs:

shiide no yama
koyuru taema wa
araji kashi
nakunaru hito no
kazu tsuzukitsutsu

There's no gap or break
In the ranks of those marching
Under the hill:
An endless line of dying men,
Moving on and on and on . . . .

Yoshino yama　　　　Last year, Yoshino,
kozo no shiori no　　I walked away bending branches
　　michi kaete　　　　　To point me to blossoms—
mada minukata no　　Which now are everywhere and I can
hana o tazunen　　　　Go where I've never been before.

　miyabashira　　　　　Shrine pillar
shitatsu iwane ni　　Rooted firmly in the rocks;
　　shikitatete　　　　　Sun in the sky
tsuyu mo kumoran　　Casting down a shaft of light
hi no mikage kana　　Never captured by cloud.

iwama tojishi	Tightly held by rocks
kōri mo kesa wa	Through winter, the ice today
tokesomete	Begins to come undone:
koke no shitamizu	A way-seeker also is the water,
michi motomuran	Melting, murmuring from the moss.

Yoshino yama	Yoshino Mountain:
sakura ga eda ni	White puffs on cherry limbs
yuki chirite	Are fallen snow,
hana osogenaru	Informing me that blossoms
toshi ni mo aru kana	Will be late this year.

sakisomuru	The first sprig just
hana o hito eda	Breaking into bloom: what if
mazu orite	I would snap it off
mukashi no hito no	To use it for memorial
tame to omowan	To someone torn away from me?

omoikaesu	Today's satori:
satori ya kyō wa	Such a change of mind would
nakaramashi	Not exist without
hana ni someoku	My lifelong habit of having
iro nakariseba	My mind immersed in blossoms.

haru o hete	For many springs
hana no sakari ni	I've come here to meet
aikitsutsu	And unite my mind
omoide ōki	With the opening blossoms—so
waga mi narikeri	I'm made of many recollections.

michinobe no	"Just a brief stop"
shimizu nagaruru	I said when stepping off the road
yanagi kage	Into a willow's shade
shibashi tote koso	Where a bubbling stream flows by . . .
tachidomaritsure	As has time since my "brief stop" began.

yoraretsuru
nomose no kusa no
    kageroite
suzushiku kumoru
yūdachi no sora

Curling in the heat,
This small field's grass blades
    Now find shelter
Under cooling clouds: night falls
With rain from the vast sky.

aware ika ni
kusaba no tsuyu no
    koboruran
akikaze tachinu
Miyagino no hara

One is moved by
Dewdrops hanging from
    Grass blades and
Now facing fall's fierce wind:
On the wide heath at Miyagino.

tsuki miba to   Tonight's moon stirs
chigiri okite shi   Memory of a pact to let
furusato no   It do this to us:
hito mo ya koyoi   Maybe she, back where we loved,
sode nurasuran   Has tear-wet sleeves like mine.

komu yo ni wa   Beyond this life and
kokoro no uchi ni This world I'll have it til
arawasan   My heart's content:
akade yaminuru   The bright moon that passed over
tsuki no hikari o   The horizon before I had my fill.

hito wa kode
kaze no keshiki mo
fukenuru ni
aware ni kari no
otozurete yuku

The one expected
Doesn't come and the moaning wind
   Tells the night is late;
A sound outside deepens loneliness:
Geese, calling, fly past.

kirigirisu
yozamu ni aki no
naru mama ni
yowaru ka koe no
tōzakari yuku

As each night of fall
Grows colder than the one before,
   The chirp of the cricket
Gets more feeble: each night it
Moves farther into the distance.

tsuki o matsu   In early winter's rain
takane no kumo wa   I'm pleased when up at the peak
harenikeri   Clouds spread open
kokoro arubeki   To show me the moon I longed to see:
hatsushigure kana   A storm that knows compassion.

A winter poem:

yamagawa ni   On a mountain stream,
hitori hanarete   A mandarin duck made single
sumu oshi no   By loss of its mate
kokoro shiraruru   Now floats quietly over ripples:
nami no ue kana   A frame of mind I know.

haruka naru	Boulder-encircled
iwa no hazama ni	Empty space, so far away that
hitori ite	Here I'm all alone:
hitometsutsu made	A place where man can't view me
monoomowabaya	But I can review all things.

ariake wa	The moon as dawn breaks
omoide are ya	Glides freely through thick clouds,
yokogumo no	Layer on layer:
tadayowaretsuru	Then strata of the past as well
shinonome no sora	One by one open before my mind.

Written when I was petitioning Retired Emperor Toba to grant me his permission to leave secular life:

oshimu tote
oshimarenubeki
    kono yo kawa
mi o sutete koso
mi o mo tasukeme

So loath to lose
What really should be loathed:
    One's vain place in life,
We maybe rescue best the self
Just by throwing it away.

kore ya mishi
mukashi sumiken
    ato naran
yomogi ga tsuyu ni
tsuki no yadoreru

Can it be just this
That remains of my earlier
    Stay here:
The moon dwelling in a dewdrop
Hung on wormwood in a waste?

At the time that the priest Jakunen invited others to contribute verses to a hundred-poem collection, I declined to take part. But then on the road where I was making a pilgrimage to Kumano, I had a dream. In it appeared Tankai, the administrator of Kumano, and [the poet] Shunzei. Tankai said to Shunzei: "Although all things in this world undergo change, the Way of Poetry extends unaltered even to the last age." I opened my eyes and understood. Then I quickly wrote a verse and sent it off to Jakunen. This is what I composed there in the heart of the mountains:

sue no yo no	"Even in an age
kono nasake nomi	Gone bad the lyric's Way
kawarazu to	Stays straight"—
mishi yume nakuba	Not seeing this in a dream,
yoso ni kikamashi	I'd have been deaf to truth.

I grew tired of living on Mount Kōya and went to a mountain temple at a place called Futami in the area of Ise. The sacred mountain of the great Shinto shrine there is referred to as the mountain traversed by sacred beings. Reflecting on the fact that the Great Goddess Amaterasu, who is worshiped at the imperial shrine in Ise, is a manifest expression of Dainichi Buddha, I composed the following:

fukaku irite
kamiji no oku o
   tazunureba
mata ue mo naki
mine no matsukaze

Following the paths
The gods passed over, I seek
   Their innermost place;
Up and up to the highest of all:
   Peak where wind passes through pines.

Seeing the moon at Tsukiyomi Shrine [at Ise]:

sayaka naru
Washi no takane no
   kumoi yori
kage yawaraguru
Tsukiyomi no mori

Over Vulture Peak
There in Buddha's time and place:
   A bedazzling moon,
Here softly filtered into
Tsukiyomi sacred shrine.

It was when I heard that the capital had been moved to Fukuhara and while I was at Ise that I wrote the following about the moon:

kumo-no-ue ya   "Above-the-Cloud-Ones":
furuki miyako to   A name for courtiers of a capital
   narinikeri   Which once was;
sumuran tsuki no   A fact about the brilliant moon
kage wa kawarade   Which, unchanging, still is.

While in the far north to visit people I knew there, I was at Saya-no-naka yama [Mount Dead-o'-Night] and I remembered the past:

toshi takete   Little did I guess
mata koyubeshi to   I'd ever pass either so many
   omoiki ya   Years . . . or this mountain
inochi narikeri   Again in one, now long, life:
Saya-no-naka yama Over Mount Dead-o'-Night!

While undertaking religious exercises in the eastern region, I wrote the following in view of Mount Fuji:

kaze ni nabiku The wisps of smoke from Fuji
Fuji no keburi no Yield to the wind and lose themselves
sora ni kiete In sky, in emptiness—
yukue mo shiranu Which takes as well the aimless passions
waga omoi kana That through my life burned deep inside.

Tsu no kuni no Famed for its springtime,
Naniwa no haru wa Naniwa in Tsu, seen today at last:
yume nare ya A field of withered reeds
ashi no kareba ni Bent down by harsh winds—my dream
kaze wataruru nari To see it come false . . . come true.

yama fukaku　　　By imagining
sakoso kokoro wa　These mountain depths, some men think
　kayou tomo　　　　They come and go here;
sumade aware o　　But, not living here themselves,
shiran mono kawa　Can they know real pathos?

yo o sutsuru　　　　So, then, it's the one
hito wa makoto ni　Who has thrown his self away
　sutsuru ka wa　　　Who is thought the loser?
sutenu hito koso　　But he who cannot lose self
sutsuru narikere　　Is the one who has really lost.

> *yamazato ni*
> *ukiyo itowan*
> *hito mo gana*
> *kuyashiku sugishi*
> *mukashi kataran*

> Here in these mountains
> I'd like one other who turned
> His back to the world:
> We'd go on about the useless way
> We spent our days when in society.

> *mukashi mishi*
> *niwa no komatsu ni*
> *toshi furite*
> *arashi no oto o*
> *kozue ni zo kiku*

> A garden sapling
> When long ago I saw this pine—
> Now so grown, its high
> Branches in their soughing tell
> Time goes and a storm comes.

izuku ni mo
sumarezuba tada
   sumade aran
shiba no iori no
shibashi naru yo ni

Nowhere is there place
To stop and live, so only
   Everywhere will do:
Each and every grass-made hut soon leaves
Its place within this withering world.

hana sakishi
Tsuru-no-hayashi no
   sono kami o
Yoshino no yama no
kumo ni mishi kana

I saw in Yoshino's
Billows of blossoms that long-ago
   Time of Great Passing
When the śāla trees surrounding Him
Suddenly turned as white as cranes.

Bibliography
and Index of First Lines

Sources in Japanese

Watanabe Tamotsu, *Sanka-shū zenchūkai*
Kubota Shōichirō, *Saigyō no Kenkyū*
Kobayashi Hideo, "Saigyō" in *Kobayashi Hideo zenshū*, vol. 8
Kubota Jun, *Shinkokin Kajin no Kenkyū*
Kawada Jun, *Saigyō no Den to Uta*
Yasuda Ayao, *Saigyo*
Yasuda Ayao, *Saigyō to Teika*
Yasuda Ayao, *Uta no fukasa*
Ueda Miyoji, *Saigyō, Sanetomo, Ryōkan*
Ishida Yoshisada, *Chūsei Sōan no bungaku*
Ishida Yoshisada, *Inja no bungaku*
Sasaki Yukitsuna, *Chūsei no Kajintachi*
Kazamaki Keijirō, *Saigyō to Kenkō*
Yamamoto Kenkichi [taidanshū] *Shizen to Geijutsu*
Kamei Katsuichirō, *Nihonjin no Seishinshi*, vol. 3
Ienaga Saburō, *Nihon shisōshi ni okeru Shūnyōteki Shizenkan no
    Tenkai*
Mezaki Tokue, *Hyōhaku*
Kaishaku to Kanshō, vol. 6 (1976): "Saigyō to Teika"

The following index lists first lines in both romaji and English
translation, numbered according to the *Nihon koten zensho* edition
of the *Sanka-shū* (abbreviated SKS), as well as the *Shinkokin-shū*
(SKKS) wherever applicable. It should be noted, however, that the
romaji is generally adopted from the former of these two
anthologies.